Publisher's Note

We have chosen to publish this beautiful notebook as it appeared in its Egyptian version, as a book to be read from right to left. This is why the front cover is where the back cover would normally be. In keeping with the Arabic pictorial tradition in which calligraphy is an integral part of the work, the Arabic text appears as part of the art, as it did in the original notebook, and the English translation appears in the margins.

The Illustrator's Notebook was conceived by Egyptian artist Mohieddin Ellabbad, who is passionately interested in perspective — his own, first and foremost, but also that which serves as a vehicle for our culture. Each page of this book is a source of discovery and surprise as it explores different ways of seeing things.

Open this book and read it as its creator intended, and learn to see things in a new way.

Preface

With his drive for precision and quality, Mohieddin Ellabbad has been exasperating book publishing professionals in Egypt and abroad for more than thirty years. He stands almost six feet tall, but printers have nicknamed him Mister Millimeter! Yet everyone agrees that by never sacrificing quality, and by always preserving an artisan's integrity and dignity, he has almost single-handedly reinvented the Arabic tradition of graphic art.

The words that come to mind when I think of Mohieddin are scholarly and imaginative, and on a personal level, graceful, especially when it comes to the heart.

Farouk Mardam-Bey
Minister of Culture,
Institut du Monde Arabe

Groundwood Books / House of Anansi Press
110 Spadina Avenue, Suite 801
Toronto, Ontario M5V 2K4

Distributed in the USA by Publishers Group West
1700 Fourth Street, Berkeley, CA 94710

Library and Archives Canada Cataloguing in Publication

Ellabbad, Mohieddin
The Illustrator's Notebook / by Mohieddin Ellabbad.
Translation of: Le carnet du dessinateur

ISBN-13: 978-0-88899-700-5 – ISBN-10: 0-88899-700-0

1. Ellabbad, Mohieddin – Notebooks, sketchbooks, etc. – Juvenile literature. 2. Ellabbad, Mohieddin – Childhood and youth – Juvenile literature. 3. Illustrators – Egypt – Biography – Juvenile literature. I. Title.

NC993.E392E4413 2006   j741.6'42'092   C2005-905322-4

Mohieddin Ellabbad

The Illustrator's Notebook

Groundwood Books / House of Anansi Press
Toronto   Berkeley

Souvenirs

I have always saved bits and pieces of things. They may seem unimportant, but these objects help me remember past times in my life. When I look at them, the old days come alive again, right down to the smallest detail. On this page I've put some of the things that I've managed to save.

Souvenirs awaken our memories and bring them to life. Without memories, we would have no past.

The world around us is filled with all kinds of souvenirs — from the huge to the very small — pyramids, the sphinx, old buildings, beautiful art found in museums and libraries, even the little things like the ones on this page. They bring the past back to life — not just our own personal past, but the very ancient past of the whole world.

منذ أيام الطفولة، وأنا أحتفظ بعدد من التذكارات الصغيرة التي تبدو ساذجة. لكن رؤيتي لها كثيرًا ما تجعلني أتذكر فترات مضت من العمر نبقى صيلها الرائعة. وعند ذلك تحضر الأيام الماضية أمامي حية زاخرة. وفي هذه الصفحة، أقدم بعض ما أحتفظ به من تذكارات صغيرة.

والتذكارات تحيي الذاكرة وتنشطها، ولولا ذاكرتنا الحية النشطة لفقدت الأيام الماضية الحياة، ولأصبحت غير موجودة.

ويمكننا أن نعتبر الكثير من المعالم الهامة في الدنيا أنواعًا من التذكارات: فالأهرام وأبو الهول والعمائر القديمة، وما تضمه المتاحف ودور الكتب، كلها (وإن كانت ضخمة) أيضًا تذكارات تحيي الزمان البعيد في ذاكرتنا من جديد!

ذكارات الحياة

4

تعودت منذ مدة طويلة أن أجمع الصور على اختلاف أنواعها، وأصبح عندي منها الآن مجموعة كبيرة . وعندما أتفرج على مجموعتي، أستطيع أن «أشم» رائحة خاصة للمنظر الذي تمثله كل صورة منها !

هذه الصورة أشم فيها رائحة ماء الورد

وهنا أجد رائحة سوائل تنظيف الأرضيات الخشبية

ومن هنا أشم رائحة اليانسون

وأشم في هذه رائحة ثمار اللوز الأخضر مخلوطة برائحة خشب قديم مبلل بالماء

Look and smell!

For many years now I have been collecting images of all kinds. I still have many of them today. When I look through my collection, I feel that each picture has its own special smell.

(Top)
This picture smells like rose water to me.

(Black-and-white picture, victory arch)
When I look at this picture, I smell floor cleaner.

(Color picture, small port)
This one smells like anise, which is a lot like licorice.

(Black-and-white picture, mosque)
Here I smell the aroma of fresh almonds perfumed with old damp wood.

A Childhood Dream

When I was a child, I lived near the Sultan Hassan mosque. There was a streetcar that ran down the main street, and when it turned the corner by the mosque, it made a terrible noise. No one in the world seemed as important or as impressive as the conductor who drove that enormous, imposing monster.

For a long time, I dreamed of driving a streetcar. Then I grew up and wasn't able to become a streetcar driver — I don't even have a driver's license! But I did learn to draw, and I became an illustrator. I am very lucky to have found this career, because now I can draw myself as the streetcar driver I always wanted to be.

The Stupid Hen!

When I was eight years old, there was a wonderful children's magazine. Every time a new issue came out, all the kids in my family would get so excited we couldn't sleep. It felt like morning would never come, and when it finally did, we got up much earlier than usual.

I would go out to run the morning errands. When I got back to the house with the groceries for breakfast, my father's paper and the anxiously awaited magazine, my sister would be watching for me from the balcony. She'd call down to me impatiently asking what was inside, and I would yell back to her from the sidewalk.

One day I called, "There's one story that looks good. It's called *The Stupid Hen!*"

I hadn't had time to read a single word of the story, but I really liked the title. Just looking at the illustration brought all kinds of images to my mind.

I have tried to draw that illustration from memory, but my drawing isn't an exact copy of the original. The hen from my childhood was thinner, and its neck was longer.

What about you? Do you ever get impatient to read a story in a magazine or a book?

Where do stories come from?

One day, my father decided to give me all my pocket money for the month at once. He wanted to teach me to be responsible and to budget wisely. At that point in my life, I dreamed of writing my own stories and illustrating them. So I didn't do very much thinking or budgeting before I went to the stationery store and bought a little red notebook so that I could write and draw on fine paper. It was a very beautiful book to look at and to touch. It even smelled good.

I couldn't use the notebook during the day, because I knew my father would get mad at me if he found out that I'd spent all my money on one thing. I only took it out at night, when everyone else was asleep. I would look at it and touch it and dream about all the stories and all the drawings that I would entrust to my secret little notebook. But I could never actually bring myself to put anything on its pages.

To this day, I have kept my special notebook blank. Even now that I am a grownup, I still remember all the stories and pictures I dreamed of thanks to it, and I have used these stories and pictures to make real books.

في الأسبوع الماضي ، و صلتني بطاقة بريد من صديقي مسافر في بلد بعيد :
كان على البطاقة منظر من هناك لبحيرة و سفينة وجبل !

بطاقتان !

L'ARBRE DE LA SAINTE-VIERGE — MATARIEH

في اليوم نفسه ، كنت عند بائع الكتب القديمة ، و عثرت على بطاقة قديمة ، عمرها أقل قليلا من ١٠٠ عام . و دهشت ؛ فقد كان المنظر المطبوع على البطاقة الثانية لمكان أليف جدا و قريب جدا بالنسبة لي . لأنه ذات المكان الذي يقع فيه مرسمى الذي أعمّ فيه الآن هذا الكتاب !

تأملت المفارقة و تعجبت :
وجدت البطاقة الأولى مرسلة " من مكان إلى مكان " ، بينما الأخرى مرسلة " من زمان إلى زمان " !

Two Postcards

Last week, I received a postcard from a friend who was traveling in a country very far away. The picture on the postcard showed a lake, a boat and some mountains.

The same day, at a second-hand bookstore, I found another postcard that was almost one hundred years old. To my great surprise, I recognized the landscape on this postcard. I know it very well, because it is the place where my studio is located, right here, where I am making this very book at this very moment.

The first postcard was sent from one place to another, and the second one from one time to another. A postcard coincidence!

9

Postage Stamp

I've always enjoyed writing letters to friends who live in far-away countries. I've probably sent hundreds of letters in my life and received just as many. I was always very impatient to get letters from Karim, who lives on the Perfume Coast. His letters always had the same stamp, and even after all these years that stamp evokes a very strong reaction in me. I have drawn it here from memory.

From the comfort of my home, I would lose myself in the stamp's magical world. I was jealous that Karim lived in such a place, surrounded by such magnificent landscapes.

Later, when I became an artist and illustrator, I wrote many stories about the world that this stamp represented for me. I have used it in dozens of drawings and poems.

I never dared to dream that one day I might be able to visit Karim, that I could spend even an hour in those fantastic surroundings. Decades passed. Then one day, I was asked to visit a number of different places for work, one of them being the Perfume Coast. I was off, my heart pounding with anticipation.

I didn't see Karim when I was there because he was out of town. I rushed over to the place by the sea that I had seen on the stamp, drawn in such wonderful colors. Sadly, I discovered that it was not so extraordinary. It looked very much like a thousand other places. There was nothing very magical about it at all!

Once I recovered from my disappointment, my sadness disappeared like a cloud blown away by the wind. I sat down and wrote to Karim. I thanked him for all the dreams he had given me with his letters and their stamps. Without them, I would never have imagined all those stories, I would never have written all those poems, and I would never have created all those drawings.

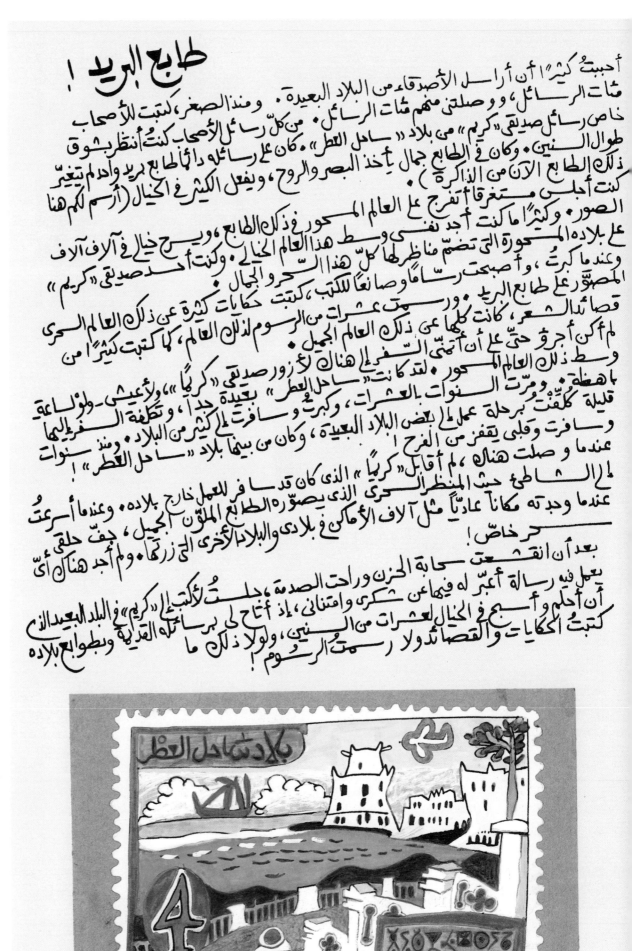

Discoveries

One day, I had nothing in particular to do. Relaxed, my mind at rest, I just sat in my studio passing the time. I found myself gazing intently at an Egyptian ten-pound note. Magnificent! I saw things that I had never noticed before, even though I'd been using these bills for years. There was a picture of the Ar-Rifaï mosque in Cairo, with a big chandelier, a marble platform for the readings from the Koran, small glass lamps and all sorts of calligraphic decorations. On the other side of the bill there was a portrait of a pharaoh with pyramids in the background. There were also flocks of geese, pelicans and other birds, surrounded by hieroglyphics and strange symbols. One of them is this two-legged jar.

There are thousands of things around us that we don't even see, because we don't take the time to look at them. For example, have you ever looked at the beautiful landscape that is drawn right in the palm of your hand?

First Impression

Once I was all alone in the middle of a big field by my grandfather's house. Suddenly, the huge shadow of an airplane slid across the earth, completely engulfing me before it raced away at lightning speed, chasing after the plane that was soaring through the air above me.

A shiver of pleasure went through my body. I felt like I had just received a wonderful gift. I said to myself, Maybe I will be able to travel in a plane one day!

Much time has passed since then, and I've grown up. Although I often travel by air now, I always look out the window to follow the shadow of the plane on the ground. And I always try to see the children that the shadow skims over. Are they also dreaming of traveling one day?

أوَّلُ لَـمْـسَـة !

كنتُ أَقِفُ وحيدًا في حقلِ جدّي الرّحبِ ، حين فوجئتُ بظلِّ هائلٍ لطائرةٍ ركابٍ ينزلقُ سريعًا على أرضِ الحقلِ ، ويلفُّني حتّى يغطّيني ، ثمّ يهربُ في لمحِ البرقِ ملاحقًا الطائرةَ الضّخمةَ التي تسبحُ فوقنا في السّماءِ ، وننفضى سريعتها .

شعرتُ برعدةٍ جميلةٍ تهزُّ جسمي ، وسعدتُ بهذه المصادفةِ النّادرةِ ، واعتبرتها امتيازًا كبيرًا فزتُ به ، وقلتُ لنفسي : لعلّ فرصة ركوبِ الطائرةِ تقتربُ منّي ! وبقيتُ أحلمُ بالسّفرِ !

ومرّت الأيامُ ، وكبرتُ ، وسافرتُ على الطائرةِ عدّةَ مرّاتٍ ، ولا زلتُ ، من شبّاكِ الطائرةِ ، أتابعُ ظلّها وهو ينزلقُ على الأرضِ بنفسى سريعتها ، وأحاول بكلّ جهدي أن أرى هؤلاء الصّغارَ الذين يلمسُهم ظلّ الطائرةِ ويجعلهم يحلمون بالسّفرِ .

The Artist and the Flowers

A few years ago, when I was very anxious and unhappy, I was asked to draw a bush with seven flowers on it for a counting book. You can see my illustration at the top of this page.

Time passed, and I found relief from my anxiety and worries. Feeling much easier, I looked back at that drawing, and I didn't like it at all. I sat down at my drawing table to do the same illustration again.

Here is the new picture. Can you see the difference?

منذ عدّة سنوات ، مرّت بي أوقات لم أكن فيها مرتاح البال ، وكنتُ قلقاً منقبض النفس . كان عليّ في ذلك الوقت أن أرسم شجيرة بها سبع زهورٍ في كتاب عن «الأعداد» ، وكان هذا الرسم [أعلى] .

دار الزمن ، و استطعت أن أتخلّص من ذلك الانقباض والقلق وارتاح بالي أكثر ، وعندما عدتُ لأتفرج على رسمتُ لم يُعجبني أبداً ، فجلستُ و رسمتُ رسماً جديداً للفكرة نفسها . وهاهو نفسها . وهاهو الرسم الجديد ←

هل تستطيع أن تتبيّن الفرق بين هذين الرسمين ؟

Cats

Here are drawings of cats from many different countries. Some are very recent, while others are hundreds, even thousands of years old. Their creators are famous artists, except for one, which was drawn by an unknown child. All of these cats are different, and all of them are beautiful.

When I was younger, I looked at all of these drawings to decide how I should draw a cat. Years have passed, and I have learned one very important thing.

I have had to forget about all these cats in order to draw my cat, the cat that I know, the cat that lives in my world. My cat may be different from all the others, but it will be my very own cat!

عندما كنّا صغارًا، كنا نبهر بالرسوم المطبوعة في الكتب والمجلات، وندهش للإتقان الفائق فيها، وكنا نسمّيها «رسوم المطبعة». وعندما كنا نحب برسم بارع لأحدنا، ونريد أن نمتدحه، كنا نقول:

«إنه عبقري يرسم مثل المطبعة!»

وكان حلم كلٍّ منا أن نرسم مثل المطبعة.

كبرنا وعرفنا بعض الأشياء: عرفنا أن المطبعة هي مجرد آلة صمّاء لا ترسم، ولكنها تطبع ما يقدمه لها الرسّام: سواء أكان رسمًا بارعًا متقنًا، أو رسمًا غير ذلك. وعرفنا أن الرسّام الحقيقي يرسم «مثلما يحب أن يرسم»، وليس «مثلما ترسم المطبعة». فالمطبعة تستطيع له ما يرسمه مهما كان الرسم.

How should we draw?

When I was little, my friends and I marveled at the drawings that were printed in books and magazines. We thought they were beautiful, and we called them "printing press pictures." When one of us did a good drawing, we would compliment him by saying, "Wow, he's really good! He can draw just like a printing press!" We dreamed of being able to draw that well.

Here is an old illustration from *Alice's Adventures in Wonderland*, a book by Lewis Carroll, an example of what we would call "a printing press picture."

When we grew up, we learned a thing or two. For example, we discovered that a printing press is just a lifeless machine. It doesn't create art. It just reproduces the images presented to it, whether they are beautiful or not. We learned that the true artist draws "what he likes to draw" and not "like a printing press." It's the other way around. A printing press will print what the artist has drawn. Without the artist it is nothing.

Draw a wolf!

What do artists do when they have to draw a wolf and they want to remember what a wolf looks like?

Some artists remember the wolves that they've seen at the zoo or in a movie or on television or maybe even in a photograph or in paintings by other artists…

Others might think about what they were told about wolves when they were little, about fairy tales, about dreams they had…

Other artists go even deeper into a memory, hidden within themselves, of when people were cave people who lived among wolves and had to fight them with their bare hands or with crude weapons.

A good artist is the one who can mix up all these different memories and pieces of information so that what his pencil conjures up is a real wolf, a beautiful wolf. But don't expect it to look like the wolves that we see in photographs or textbooks!

بعد ما كبرنا قليلاً ، تعلمنا أسماء أنواع كثيرة من الألوان. تعلمنا أن الأزرق ليس "أزرق" واحداً ، وأن هناك عشرات الأنواع من "الأحمر" و "الأصفر" و "الأخضر". كما تعلمنا أن هناك أنواعاً كثيرة من الألوان الأخرى غير المعروفة.

في تلك الفترة البعيدة ، تعرفنا على لون اسمه "لون بشرة الجسم". كنا نشتريه جاهزاً على شكل معجون معبأ في أنابيب، أو سائل في زجاجات ، وكنا - جميعاً - نستعمله في تلوين الوجوه والأيدي والأجسام البشرية. ولم ينتبه أحدنا - في ذلك الوقت - إلى أن تلك الألوان كانت تصنع في أوروبة وأمريكا وتصدّر إلى بلادنا، وبالتالي لم ننتبه أيضاً إلى أن من صنعوا ذلك اللون إنما صنعوه لا ستعمالهم، ولذا فهو يشبه

لون بشرتهم هم.

وفي يوم، وبينما أرسم، نظرت إلى يدي التي تمسك بفرشاة الرسم وتلوّن الأجسام بذلك اللون الجاهز، فوجدت فرقاً هائلاً! كان لون بشرة يدي يختلف كثيراً عن لون البشرة الذي أستعمله في التلوين! تعجبت وتوقفت عن التلوين، ثم توقفت بعدها عن استعمال ذلك اللون، وبدأت أتعلم كيف أكوّن بنفسي لوناً جديداً للوجوه والأيدي والسيقان والأجسام يماثل لون بشرتي وبشرة أهلي!

My Color

When we were children, we learned the names of all the colors. We were taught that there were dozens of different shades of red, yellow and green, as well as many other colors that we'd never heard of.

Back then, we discovered a color that was called "flesh pink." We would buy it in a little tube or bottle. Everyone used it to color the faces, hands and bodies of the people we drew. We didn't pay attention to the fact that these tubes of paint came from Europe or North America. These paints were sold in our country, but the people who manufactured them made the paints for themselves, to match the color of their skin.

One day as I was painting, my gaze fell on my hand holding the paintbrush that I was using to color in my characters. Suddenly, the difference seemed so obvious! My skin was not at all the same color! Surprised, I stopped what I was doing and then actually stopped using this color of paint altogether. I learned to mix my own paint, especially for faces, hands, legs and bodies. It is the color of my skin and the skin of my people.

Left and Right

Here's something that I didn't learn when I was little and that no adult ever explained to me.

When I got older, I discovered this very simple thing, something that had never even occurred to me before.

I realized that in Arabic-speaking countries (as well as in some others), we read and write from right to left, and we draw and look at pictures in the same direction.

People in countries that use the Roman and Cyrillic alphabets, for example, draw and look at things from left to right, which is how they read and write (and think).

The pictures that appeal to us in my part of the world are the ones that go in the same direction as the way we read. In these drawings the eye moves from right to left, and figures move from right to left if they are leaving, and in the opposite direction if they are arriving.

I haven't really thought about how Arab people dream, but I think that we must even dream from right to left!

18

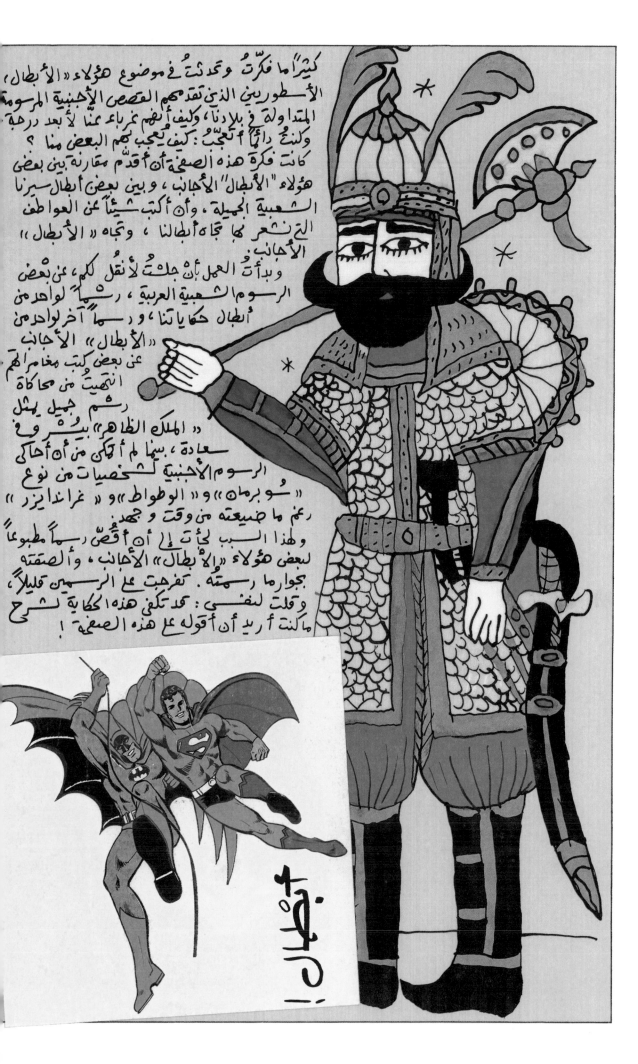

Heros

I often think about comic book characters from other countries, these so-called heros. Every time, I ask myself the same question. Why do we like them?

On this page, I wanted to compare these comic book heros to the characters from our own traditional stories. I wanted to do two drawings — one to illustrate one of our stories and another taken from a foreign comic book.

I finished my first drawing easily, a depiction of King Baïbars, and I really enjoyed doing it. But no matter how hard I tried or how much time I spent, I couldn't copy the pictures of characters like Superman or Batman.

So in the end, I had to cut out a picture and glue it next to my own drawing. Looking at the two images, I realized they explain exactly what I was trying to show on this page!

Upside Down

Atlases are among the most beautiful Arabic manuscripts I have ever seen.

One of the most magnificent is the Al-Idrissi atlas. (Al-Idrissi died in 1165.) He called his atlas *The Fruitful Journey to the Horizons of the Earth*. I was able to obtain color reproductions of several manuscripts, including this atlas. After examining them carefully, I discovered some surprising details. For example, the ancient Arabic cartographers always placed North at the bottom of the page and South at the top. West was to the right of the page, and East to the left! This is the exact opposite of how we are taught to draw a map in geography class.

I thought about this for a while. Then I asked myself, Why is this so surprising? Isn't the way we draw the earth just a convention? The earth isn't attached to the ceiling of a room or contained in a box, with a top and a bottom. In fact, it is surrounded by an absolute void.

When things take us by surprise, we often refuse to accept them just because they don't fit in with the ideas we already have in our heads, even if those ideas turn out to be inaccurate.

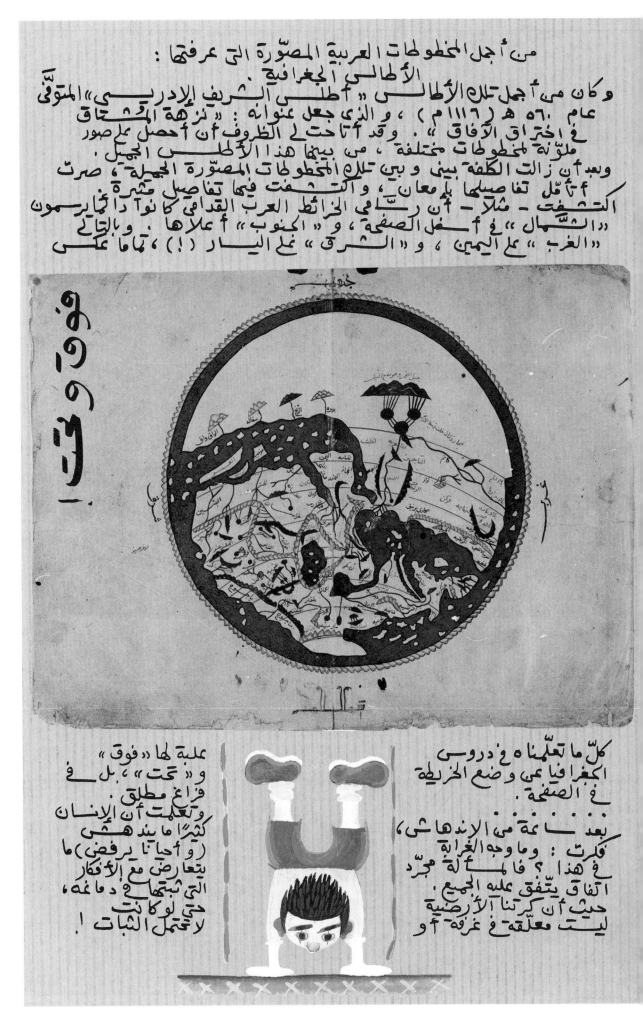

من أجمل المخطوطات العربية المصوّرة التي عرفتها:
الأطالس الجغرافية.
وكان من أجمل تلك الأطالس "أطلس الشريف الإدريسي" المتوفّى
عام ٥٦٠ هـ (١١١٦ م)، والذي جعل عنوانه: "نزهة المشتاق
في اختراق الآفاق". وقد أتاحت لي الظروف أن أحصل على صور
ملوّنة لمخطوطات مختلفة، من بينها هذا الأطلس الجميل.
وبعد أن زالت الكلفة بيني وبين تلك المخطوطات المصوّرة الجميلة، صرت
أتأمّل تفاصيلها بإمعان، واكتشفت فيها تفاصيل مثيرة
للدهشة - مثلاً - أن رسّامي الخرائط العرب القدامى كانوا دائماً يرسمون
"الشمال" في أسفل الصفحة، و"الجنوب" أعلاها. وبالتالي
"الغرب" على اليمين، و"الشرق" على اليسار (!)، تماماً عكس

كلّ ما تعلّمناه في دروس
الجغرافيا عمّا في وضع الخريطة
في الصفحة.

بعد نأمة من الاندهاش،
فكّرت: وما وجه الغرابة
في هذا؟ فالمسألة مجرّد
اتفاق يتّفق عليه الجميع.
حيث أن كرتنا الأرضية
ليست معلّقة في غرفة أو

علبة لها "فوق"
و"تحت"، بل في
فراغ مطلق.
وتعلّمت أن الإنسان
كثيراً ما يندهش
(أو أحياناً يرفض) ما
يتعارض مع الأفكار
التي شبّها في دماغه،
حتى لو كانت
لا تحتمل الثبات!

السُّلطان..

.. وأنا!

لم يكُن السلاطين الأتراك يوقّعون أسماءهم مثل باقي خلق الله، فقد كان الخطّاطون العظام قد اخترعوا طرقاً فريدة لكتابة اسم كل سلطان منهم.

سُمّيت طريقة توقيع السلطان بـ«الطُّغراء». وكانت تشكيلاً جميلاً من خط «الثُّلُث» تتشابك فيه الحروف، وترتفع من بينها ثلاثة من حروف «الألف» مثل الرايات، ويُختم اسم السلطان بكلمة «خان»، ثم بوصف «المظفّر دائماً».

أعجبتني طريقة توقيع السلاطين سنوات طويلة، وحاولت تقليدها مراراً. وأخيراً تصوّرت أني قد نجحت عندما كتبت اسمي هكذا:

تفرّجتُ على اسمي مكتوباً بهذه الطريقة العجيبة، فوجدته ركيكاً بل ومضحكاً! وتأملتُ المسألة، فعرفتُ السبب. فأنا لا «سلطان» ولا «خان»، كما أنني لستُ «مظفّراً دائماً». ألقيتُ الطُّغراء التي رسمتُها هكذا، وخرجتُ بعد، وكتبتُ

مُحيي الدين اللبّاد

The Sultan… and Me

Ottoman sultans didn't sign their names like mere mortals. Instead, the most respected calligraphers invented extraordinary signatures just for them.

This signature, particular to each sultan, was called the *tughra*, an elegant variation on a style of writing known as *thuluth*. Three letters are drawn with great flourishes, standing out from the other intertwined letters that surround them. The name of the sultan ends with the word *khan* or ruler, followed by the expression "always victorious."

For a long time, I was filled with wonder by these sultans' signatures and I tried to imitate them. (See the *tughra* at the bottom of the page.)

Looking at my name written in this strange calligraphy, I found the result clumsy, ugly, even a bit comical. I thought about it and finally understood why. I am neither a sultan, nor a khan and, most of all, I am not "always victorious."

I threw the *tughra* into the bottom of a drawer and signed my name again. You can see my signature in the white box at the bottom of this page.

21

Tasteful Writing

Sometimes the great calligraphers presented verses of the Koran and other texts in a special shape. On this page you can see a pear created by Sheik Abdel-Aziz Ar-Rifaï in 1924 from the phrase *bismillah, ar-rahmân ar-rahîm* (In the name of God, mild and merciful).

As soon as I saw this charming pear drawn in black ink, I was under its spell. When I look at it, I see it as if it is in color — shiny, fragrant, juicy and deliciously crunchy.

Every time I see a pear, I think of Sheik Ar-Rifaï, and every time I see beautiful calligraphy, I think of the pear!

And every time I bite into a pear, I say, a bit more loudly than I usually do when I am about to eat something, "In the name of God, mild and merciful."

A Wish Granted

When you're feeling good and relaxed, you are more sensitive to the magic of the art that you see, to its originality, to its power to make you feel and think. Sometimes you even want to enter this magical universe and live there, if only for a moment.

When I saw this photograph from the village of Qurna, near Luxor in the south of Egypt, I felt like this house, so full of life with the marvelous landscape painted on its walls, had been transformed into an immense painting. A painting with windows and a door that you could knock on and enter. Inside, maybe you'd find a comfortable bed where you could lie down and laze about.

Just imagine the dreams you would have surrounded by such beautiful paintings!

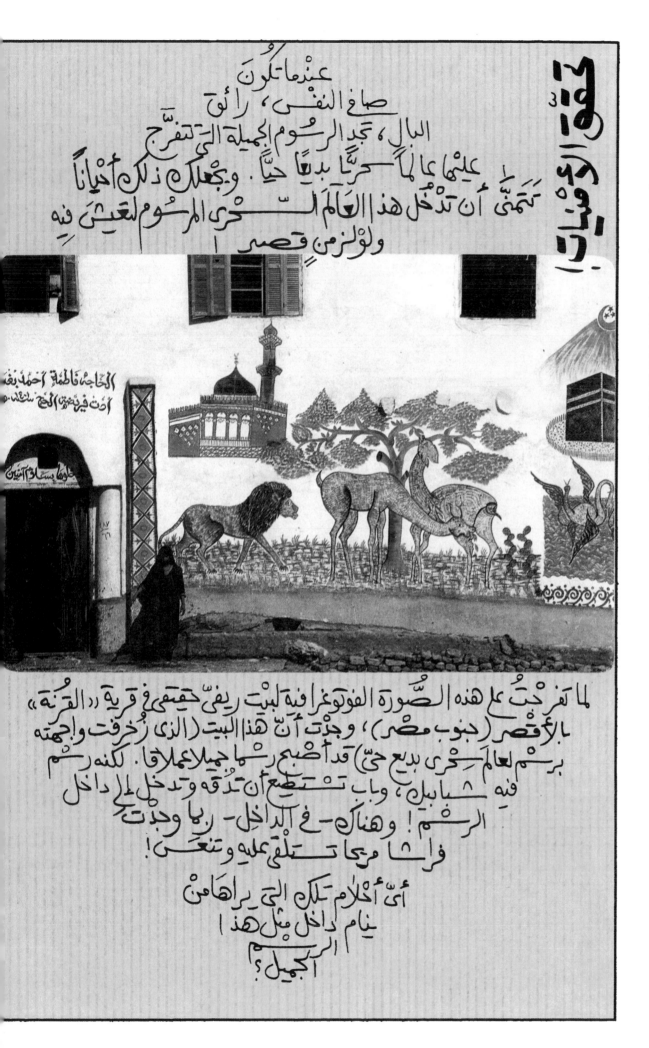

The Palm Tree's Memory

Have you ever heard about the children from Harraniya, a sleepy little town in the shadow of the pyramids? They create tapestries that depict themselves, their families and scenes of village life complete with animals, birds, the sky and the air. Their artwork is original and full of color and, most surprisingly, seems to be inspired by their ancestors from thousands of years before. But no one taught them to make these tapestries, and these children have probably never seen the work of the ancient Egyptians.

Question: How did these children come to hold in their imaginations the artistic inheritance of their ancestors? How did they find this way to express themselves? Who taught them this art form?

Answer: Does a palm tree need to be told that it is a palm tree? Does someone need to explain to it how to grow dates?

النَّخْلة!

هل سَمِعْتُمْ عَنْ «سِجّاد الحَرّانيّة» الذي يُبْدِعُهُ أطفال هذه القَرْيَة التي تنامُ في حِضْنِ أهْرام مِصْر؟ على هذا السِّجاد الجميل نَرى هؤلاء الأطفال أنْفُسَهُم، و أهْلَهُم، و حياتَهُم اليَوْميّة، و يُصَوِّرون مَشاهِد قَرْيَتِهم وحَيَواناتِها و طُيورَها و أشْجارَها و سَماءَها وهواءَها في ألْوان مُبْهِجة و أشْكال بديعة. والمُدْهِشُ أننا نلمَسُ في رُسومهم نفْسَ الرُّوح التي مَيَّزَت رُسومَ أجْدادهم مُنذ آلاف السِّنين! رغمَ أنَّ أحدًا لم يُعلِّمهُم هذا الفَنّ، و لم يُطْلِعهُم على رُسومَ أجْدادهم مِنْ قبل . . . . !

A Welcoming Book

When we visit friends, they throw open their doors, crying, "Welcome! Thank you for honoring us with your visit. You are so dear to our hearts! Your arrival brings light and illumination to our home."

Years ago, Arabic books also welcomed their readers. The first page that the reader saw would say, "Welcome! Thank you for honoring this book by reading it. Your eyes warm my heart. This book is illuminated by your gaze."

In the same way that a welcoming host anticipates the slightest need of his visitor by presenting him with candies, cool drinks, tea or coffee, special care was taken with this first page, with attention paid to the smallest detail.

This care was taken with all kinds of books, not only the Koran or religious texts as some people think. This tradition continued until very recent years.

Why have we forgotten this beautiful tradition? Why don't we decorate the first pages of our notebooks, our books and our letters to friends to honor the person who will read them, or simply to honor ourselves?

Some Room for the Reader

Were Arabic books more beautiful in the past?

In some ways, you could say yes. The people who made books in those days demonstrated more subtlety, better manners, a greater concern for their readers. How?

They didn't use the entire page. Instead they recopied the text using only three quarters of the available page, leaving the rest completely blank. Why?

They left this blank space for the readers, giving them the entire length of the page so they could make notes as they wished: comments or criticisms, explanations, ideas that came to them as they were reading the text… Some readers wrote so many notes that the book became their book.

I drew this page in the old style, leaving a big blank space in the margin. It's up to you to fill it with your thoughts about what I have written!

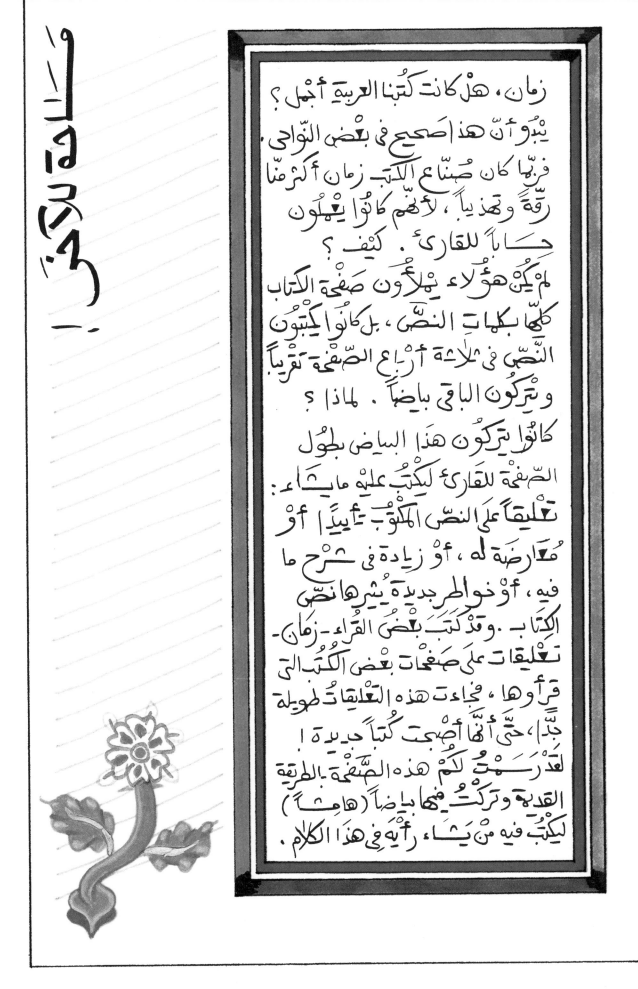

بعضُ النَّاسِ يُحِبُّونَ أَنْ يُعَلِّقُوا عَلَى حَوائِطِ بُيوتِهِم لَوْحاتٍ وَرُسومًا جَميلَةً، أَوْ أَنْ يَرْتَدوا مَلابِسَ عَلَيْها رُسومٌ مُلَوَّنَةٌ، أَوْ أَنْ يَضَعُوا عَلَى مَوائِدِهِمْ أَغْطِيَةً مَنْقوشَةً بِرُسومٍ مُبْهِجَةٍ.

وَعِنْدَما سافَرْتُ إلى مَدينَةِ «الشّارِقَة» في العامِ الماضي، زُرْتُ صَديقي هُناكَ. وَعِنْدَما دَخَلَتْ أُخْتُهُ الصَّغيرَةُ لِتُرَحِّبَ بِضَيْفِ أَخيها، وَجَدْتُها لا تَكْتَفي بِتَعْليقِ لَوْحاتِ الرَّسْمِ الجَميلَةِ، وَلا بِالمَلابِسِ والأَغْطِيَةِ المَرْسومَةِ والمَنْقوشَةِ وَغَيْرِ ذَلِكَ، بَلْ وَجَدْتُها وَقَدْ نَقَشَتْ كَفَّيْها وَقَدَمَيْها بِالحِنّاءِ لِتَكونَ هِيَ نَفْسُها لَوْحَةً مَرْسومَةً جَميلَةً! يا اللهَ!

A Living Painting!

There are people who hang paintings on the walls of their homes, who wear clothes with colorful designs or who cover their tables with brightly patterned tablecloths.

Last year, I went to Sharjah in the United Arab Emirates to visit a friend. His younger sister came to join us. That's when I discovered that paintings, clothing and beautiful cloth were not enough for her. Her hands and feet were also covered with henna designs. She had become a living painting!

The Fool

In many of our stories, both ancient and modern, you will find a fool.

In some cases, the fool is a stupid character, like in the story where the fool asks his son, "Do you remember when we last went to the mosque for Friday prayers?"

The son, who has inherited his father's stupidity, answers, "It was Wednesday, if I remember correctly!"

Other times, the fool is not stupid at all! Have you noticed that we invent characters who have all the worst faults so that we can convince ourselves that we don't suffer from the same faults? As if we weren't fools ourselves from time to time! I have to say, I think that this character resembles me in more than a few ways!

And you? What do you think?

قصة الحكايات

في كثير من حكاياتنا القديمة والحديثة توجد شخصيّة "الأحمق".

و في بعض تلك الحكايات يبدو الأحمق غبيًا، مثل تلك الحكاية التي يسأل فيها الأحمق الشهير "هبنقة" ابنه:

ـ هل تذكر متى كانت آخر مرّة صلّينا فيها الجمعة؟

فيردّ الابن الذي ورث حماقته عن أبيه:

ـ أظنّ أنها كانت يوم الأربعاء الماضي!

و في بعض الحكايات نكتشف أنّ "الأحمق" ليس غبيًا بالمرّة، وأنّه صاحب حكمة وبصيرة.

ألا ترون أننا نحبّ أن نبتكر شخوصا نحمّلها كلّ نواقصنا لنوهم أنفسنا أننا نخلو من هذه النواقص؟

فأنا مثلا نبتكر شخصية "الأحمق" ونجعله يتفرّغ للحماقة ويتخصّص فيها، ونلعبه هذا الدور بالغة وكأننا نخلو تماما من الحماقة!

أنا شخصيًا، أجد أنّ هذا الأحمق يشبهني في أشياء كثيرة.

و أنت؟

Signature

The great Arabic calligraphers were very simple, humble people. (True humility, by the way, is found only in people who respect themselves and know their true worth.) Even when these calligraphers became famous, they signed their works first with their names, then with a sentence filled with modesty. This is the case for one of the greatest of them all, Hamid Al-Amidi, who described himself in these terms: "the miserable, the hardworking, he who recognizes his weaknesses and deficiencies." Al-Amidi was also careful always to mention the name of the person who taught him the art of calligraphy. For example, in his signature on this page, he writes: "Student of Mohammad Nazif, may God forgive him his sins and erase his faults!"

This way of signing his work made a great impression on me. When it came time to sign my first drawing, this is how I wrote my name:

"By the miserable, the hardworking, he who recognizes his weaknesses and deficiencies. Mohieddin Ellabbad, student of master Khalil Mourad, former art teacher at the Qoubba Secondary School. October 1986-Mouharram 1407."

My portrait, as drawn by my son, Ahmad Ellabbad (woodcut, 1986).

My given name is Mohammad Mohieddin Moussa Ellabbad. I was born near the citadel in Old Cairo in 1940.

I studied painting at the Academy of Fine Arts in Cairo between 1957 and 1962, but after I completed my degree I was primarily interested in illustrating for magazines and newspapers.

During my years at secondary school, I worked as an illustrator for newspapers and magazines. It was during my years at the Academy of Fine Arts that I got my first job, at the magazine *Sinbad*, and I also published my first children's book with Al-Maaref publishing house.

In 1962, I was hired as an illustrator for two weekly magazines, *Roz al-youssef* and *Sabah al-khayr*. Since then, I have been working as an illustrator, author and designer in Egypt and in other Arabic countries.

I have two sons. The oldest, Moustapha, has completed his university degree in economics, and Ahmad has a degree from the Academy of Fine Arts in Cairo.

• لم أُسَمَّى بالكامل هُو :
محمد محيي الدّين مُوسَى اللبّاد
• وُلدتُ بحي القلعة فى القاهرة القديمة
عام ١٩٤٠ .

• درستُ فن تصوير اللوحات فى كلية الفُنون
الجميلة بالقاهرة من ١٩٥٧ إلى ١٩٦٢ ، لكني
لم أُمارس هذا الفن بعد أيام الدراسة ، بل
اهتممتُ برسوم المجلّة للطباعة .

• عملتُ منذ سنوات الدراسة الثانوية رسّاماً
فى الصّحف والمجلات . وأُثناء دراسة الفنون
الجميلة بدأتُ أول عمل لى فى مجلة « سندباد »
وأصدرتُ أول كتاب للأطفال فى « دار
المعارف ».

• فى عام ١٩٦٢ عملتُ رسّاماً فى « روز اليوسف »
و « صباح الخير » ، ومنذ ذلك الوقت وأنا
أعمل رسّاماً وكاتباً وصانعاً للكتب فى مصر
وغيرها من الدّول العربية .

• لى إبنان : أكبرهما « مصطفى » الذى يُكمل دراسته
العليا فى الإقتصاد ، و « أحمد » الذى تخرج من كلية
الفنون الجميلة .